MICHELLE L. L. FELTHAM

DISCOMBOBULATED

and Other Poems

Austin Macauley Publishers™
LONDON • CAMBRIDGE • NEW YORK • SHARJAH

Copyright © Michelle L. L. Feltham 2023

The right of Michelle L. L. Feltham to be identified as author of this work has been asserted in accordance with sections 77 and 78 of the Copyright, Designs and Patents Act 1988.

All rights reserved. No part of this publication may be reproduced, stored in a retrieval system, or transmitted in any form or by any means, electronic, mechanical, photocopying, recording, or otherwise, without the prior permission of the publishers.

Any person who commits any unauthorised act in relation to this publication may be liable to criminal prosecution and civil claims for damages.

A CIP catalogue record for this title is available from the British Library.

ISBN 9781398495951 (Paperback)
ISBN 9781398495968 (ePub e-book)

www.austinmacauley.com

First Published 2023
Austin Macauley Publishers Ltd
1 Canada Square
Canary Wharf
London
E14 5AA

Poems

POLITICS 5
- Discombobulated 6
- COVID 19 Virus 7
- The State of Our NHS 8
- Boris 9
- Parliament 10
- Prime Ministers 11
- Money 12
- They Went to Fight the War 13

THE NATURAL WORLD 15
- Pollution 16
- The Amazon 17
- Simba 18
- Busy Bees Cat 19
- Tabitha the Cat 20
- Weather 21
- Gardening 22

THE TIME OF YEAR 23
- New Year 24
- A Love Poem 25
- Heatwave 26
- Halloween 27
- Armistice 28
- Winter 29
- Christmas 30
- Christmas (II) 31
- Birthday 32

THE DEMON DRINK 33
    The Party 34
    Alcohol 35
    The New Old Woman 36
    The Old Man and His Drinking 37

REFLECTIONS 39
    The Ghost in the Mirror 40
    Chocolate 41
    Cakes 42
    Wanderlust 43
    Cruising 44
    Dreams 45
    The Dream 46
    Good v Evil 47
    Life After Death 48

POLITICS

Discombobulated

There comes a time when life gets confusing:
It's quite laughable, certainly it's amusing
When people who are supposed to be in charge of this great nation
Can't make up their minds how to govern it, quite frankly it's an irritation.
For although they say they're acting on their constituents' behalf,
That in itself is a real belly laugh.
We all know they're thinking more of themselves,
Their voters' needs and wants are put on those theoretical shelves.
With all this indecision over Brexit, we are either for or we're against:
Make up your minds. We're all tired of the bickering and all the complaints.
And deliver on the promises which have been stated,
And cease getting us all so discombobulated.

COVID 19 Virus

Measles, rubella and mumps
Are enough to make you feel down in the dumps,
Just like smallpox, chicken pox and the flu.
These ailments are lethal to people such as me and you,
But the worst by far is COVID 19:
It flies, invisible, through the air, it cannot be seen,
It causes havoc in its wake,
Disaster for disaster's sake,
Shops closing down in the street,
People frightened to go out and meet,
Businesses closing down for good,
An end to everybody's livelihoods.
We should all now say, "Enough is enough."
We'll not let this beat us, we will act tough.
So come on scientists, invent a pill
To stop everybody getting ill
From deadly spores that can't be seen,
Such as this awful virus called COVID 19.

The State of Our NHS

In 1948 our National Health Service was founded,
On caring for the sick and injured its function was grounded.
And so in time we've come to rely
On being treated and cured, you really can't deny
That but for the NHS you'd have to go private,
Which can be expensive, they charge exorbitant rates.
But gradually the waiting time has become excruciatingly long,
To see a doctor or nurse which is really quite wrong.
It seems that you have to really be at death's door
To be seen at all quickly which (to me) seems pretty poor.
But don't get me wrong,
Even though the waiting time can be long,
When you're finally seen and diagnosed
You're treated right away even if your injuries are self-imposed.
The management of staff needs to be greatly improved upon,
The NHS has been badly run since Matron has gone,
And as for the uniforms the hospital staff have to wear,
They're untidy, they're scruffy, there's been no thought or care
Put into how the staff look and are perceived
By patients and visitors and the recently bereaved.
So take heed of what I now suggest:
Bring back Matron to sort out this mess,
Take the medical profession back to when and how it worked best,
And help to sort out the crumbling state of our NHS.

Boris

The time to leave Europe has at last arrived,
Through blood, sweat and tears our government has survived,
The battle over Brexit is finally at an end,
Towards the sensible outcome the Labour voters did bend,
For they were sick to death of all the broken promises made
By Corbyn and his cronies, who took for granted that the people wouldn't be swayed
By what the majority of the British public voted for.
It feels as if we have just won the war,
So bravo, bravo and bravo again,
As our Prime Minister, may Boris always remain,
For he has remained true to his beliefs
That by leaving the EU we shall achieve
A better future for one and for all
And into a more prosperous age our great nation will be pulled.
So I'll say it again. For delivering on your Brexit plan,
Thank you Boris Johnson. You are the greatest leading man.

Parliament

Labour, Liberal and Conservative:
Surely there's another alternative,
A party that listens and takes heed
Of what their constituents really need,
Instead of all this arguing over Brexit.
I've got an idea of what might fix it:
Take notice of what the majority of people say,
Or some day soon there'll be a hefty price to pay.
For most of us want to leave Europe, not remain.
To ignore the majority would be insane,
For I firmly believe in democracy and freedom of speech:
Take that away and what will be the lesson we teach
The future generations about doing and saying what's right?
You'd be telling them they have nothing for which to fight.
So every country should have its own say
In how they run things from day to day.
Give us a party of which we can be proud
And which won't run Parliament into the ground.

Prime Ministers

Thatcher, Major, Cameron and May,
These are some of the leaders you hear about every day.
There's Asquith, Churchill, Blair and Brown,
To name but a few Prime Ministers in London town.
They've all served a term at one time or other,
Although most were useless, so why did they bother?
They seldom ever stood by what they promised,
And as for that man whose name is Boris,
With all the problems over this pandemic and Brexit,
It didn't surprise me that the poor bugger packed his bags & made a fast exit.
And so the party had a new leader by the name of Liz Truss,
Whose leadership was quickly scuppered, ground into dust.
And now comes another new leader whose name is Rishi,
He's quite good looking, some say that he is really quite dishy.
But good looks aside, is he a man whom the public can all trust?
To save our great country from the fear of going bust,
From lack of food and shortages of paid employment,
To fall at the first hurdle would be to the opposition's enjoyment.
So forget all the in-party squabbles and fights,
Putting their heads together and working on doing what's right
For this great nation as a whole:
That is Rishi Sunak's party's new goal.

Money

Money is a tool we all need in our lives
To feed us, to clothe us, to help us survive.
In this world of terror, violence and wars,
What's theirs is theirs and what's yours is yours.
But there're certain people who, unlike you and me,
Don't give a damn about those living in poverty.
So next time you see someone in need,
Don't just walk on by. Do a good deed.
Give some hope to those living in fear
Of never seeing a brighter new year
Of peace, happiness and plenty of spare change,
To be able to afford luxuries which to them would feel strange.
For everyone should be able to pay their own way
Through college, university and the humdrum life of every day,
'Cause for a child growing up without any money
It's sad, it's depressing, it's certainly not funny.
So if all the rich people in the world gave to the poor
Then perhaps that would mean there'd be an end to the devastating travesty of war.

They Went to Fight the War

Under threat of death from enemy fire
Our brave men trudged through the mire
Through trenches full of mud,
Passed soldiers dying, the stench of blood,
Bombs raining down from the sky,
Flashes of light before their eyes.
Those young soldiers were so very brave,
For although they may have been scared they knew that by fighting they would save
The lives of a nation that's happy and free,
To protect our country for people like you and me.
And when young children ask their Granddads,
"What kind of life was there to be had?"
For life must have been hard for young families during the war,
Never forget what they were all fighting for:
Liberty, justice and freedom for all.
That was and is why to arms they were called.
Of every Hitlerite they had to get rid,
To put an end to tyranny, violence and hatred.
And if ever we're in trouble from being overtaken once more,
Just remember how brave our men were when last they went to fight the war.

THE NATURAL WORLD

Pollution

For millennia there's been all this fuss
About people travelling by car, train, plane or bus.
They give off toxic gas emissions,
Dust clouds in the air obscuring our vision.
But what of all the drilling for oil,
Lethally dumping into the soil,
All the noxious, unwanted waste
We dispose of daily in our haste
To get rid of all the foul-smelling scents
So that we might breathe of a fresh, clean environment?
To rid our world of unwanted pollution
I think that I have found the perfect solution:
Cease using transport that you don't need
Walk to school or to work and soon indeed
You'll find that by putting in the extra time
To exercise daily your body and your mind.
Think of what you can do
To improve the lives of people such as me and you
And keep the traffic down to a bare minimum
For the risk of harming the environs.
'Cause if we don't act now all natural beauty will be gone:
No trees, no flowers, no animals, no birds in the sky singing their songs,
No fresh air for us all to breathe:
What future for the next generations will we leave?
For this planet of ours will eventually crumble
And into the void it will then tumble,
So to avoid all this devastation from happening,
Cease unnecessarily building properties which is the cause of most of the damaging
Pollutants in the atmosphere,
Destroying all the land that we hold dear.
So if you take heed and apply this solution,
You may yet prevent a catastrophic disaster caused by pollution.

The Amazon

A forest full of magnificent trees,
Foliage blowing in the breeze,
Animals roaming, happy and free,
It's such a wonderful sight to see.
So why destroy all this beauty?
And why not start doing our duty
To protect the world's most beautiful sight,
And stop setting all this forestation alight,
And cease burning all these marvellous trees down
So that all the animals don't have to go to ground
To escape the terror of heat and fire,
This extremely devastating, destructive pyre?
For one day soon all this natural beauty will be gone,
So please, please help to protect the Amazon.

Simba

"I was born with an extra digit on each paw,
Which is handy indeed:
I bang on my little cat door
To get my servants to pay attention when there is something I need.
And now it is time for me to go to my royal cat bed,
To close my eyes and rest my regal head,
For I know when I wake I'll be ready to go out on the prowl,
And if I am angry I'll give a fierce growl.
For I'm the king of my castle and I rule this house,
So beware all you vermin. Clear off, little mouse,
For if you squeak at me just one more time,
You're finished, you're history, for dinner you're mine.
And after I've washed you down with a couple of birds,
I'll be proud of myself 'cause I'll have had the last word.
So now you know the moral of my story is this:
Never come to me and ask for a kiss,
For it might just be the last thing that you ever do.
My name is Simba and I'm getting ready to pounce on you."

Busy Bees Cat

More than 20 years ago when this garden centre opened its doors,
A cat came strolling in one day upon her four paws,
And from that day until the present,
She's graced us all with her presence,
And even though she's lived to be the grand old age of about 23,
It's always a wonderful sight to see
Her prowling around the shrubs and the flowers.
It's always a joy to behold during opening hours
This cat whom they've named Susie,
She's such a sweet-natured little cutie.
She lets you give her a little fuss,
But walks away when it gets too much.
And even though soon there'll come a day
When you hear the sad news that Susie has passed away,
When you've finally dried your eyes
And you realise that the cat has had a good long life,
Be thankful for the knowledge that late at night,
When the garden centre is shut and there's no-one in sight,
The spirit of Susie lives on and is doing the rounds,
To make sure no disturbances can be found.
For in death as in life she'll be doing her duty
To the place that became home to that little cutie.
For Busy Bees garden centre was and is her home,
And through its departments she shall forever more roam.

Tabitha the Cat

My name is Tabitha and when I was young,
I was lithe and agile, I had so much fun.
I'd chase the squirrels and birds in the park,
I'd be up all hours, playing 'til dark.
But now I am old and my bones are all weary,
Yet I can honestly say that my life is not dreary,
For I feel like a pampered queen sat upon my throne,
Leaving the everyday chores to my servants alone.
For when I want feeding I'll stare at them 'til they bow to my every whim.
They'll try to ignore me although they know they can never win.
And as the queen of this house I like to drink out of a glass,
I'm definitely not a common moggie for I have got much more class.
And every now and then I'll allow my slaves to pet me
To show them how grateful I am I'll purr to let them know they treat me well indeed.
And now I'm asleep in my royal bed chamber,
And woe betide those who think to disturb my slumber.
So now you know why it's said that dogs have masters and cats have slaves:
We're always aloof to the love our owners have displayed,
And as for myself I am proud of the fact that
I am loved and cared for, I'm the simply purrrrrfect Tabitha cat.

Weather

Wind, rain, sleet and hail,
The sky is fiercely blowing a gale,
Thunder bolts and flashes of lightning,
I can hardly wait for the sun to be shining.
When the storm has diminished,
This bad weather will have finished,
No more worries about damage caused,
For the atrocious storm has finally paused
In its extremely bothersome destruction.
What causes its violent eruptions?
This devastating, chaotic rampage?
It's as if a great beast is in a fit of rage
Against all the beauty on the earth,
Destroying everything of worth.
So even though the weather can be strange,
I don't believe it's to do with climate change,
For those terrifying storms we've seen before,
When people and their pets don't venture outdoors
For fear of being swept away,
And never seeing another clear day.
So thanks be to God for the sun in the sky,
Warmth on my face and bright light in my eye.
I'll never again be scared of the bad weather,
I'll just be thankful for the fact that it doesn't last forever.

Gardening

Gardening should be a labour of love,
Making the garden habitable for birds to land in from skies above.
Lawnmower running, you're cutting the grass,
You want your garden to look first class.
Till the soil to make room for the seeds
And make sure you remember to clear out the weeds.
Now put into your garden an artificial pond,
Then fill it with all the fish of which you are fond.
And why not add a birdbath and table,
So all of your little flying friends will be able
To freshen up and have a bite to eat
Of birdseeds and nuts? It's a delightful treat.
And in winter when the ground starts to harden,
It's always a pleasure to see the wildlife come into your garden.

THE TIME OF YEAR

New Year

Christmas time was full of fun,
Presents galore for everyone,
But now it's finally the end of the year.
To get the party mood started with plenty of cheer,
Champagne is sparkling in those glass flutes.
Laughter abounds, which you can't refute.
Now the celebrations are underway
To see us safely into New Year's Day,
And soon the countdown to midnight will start,
So make sure you're not the first to depart.
10, 9, 8,7, 6, 5, 4, 3, 2,1:
The 'Auld Lang Syne' singing will soon have begun.
So let's all raise our voices whilst holding hands
And pray for a peaceful New Year throughout our fair lands.

A Love Poem

When Winter's gone
And Spring is here,
Birds sing their songs
So full of cheer.
And out of the ground does suddenly appear
Every flower and plant that we hold dear,
For every single thing in the earth
May have died, but was granted rebirth.
Baby animals such as ducklings and lambs
Are born into the world to graze the land,
And every man, woman, boy and girl
Must protect the creatures that roam the world.
For although there's chaos, famine and wars,
Kindness can be found in hearts like mine and yours.
If we all were kind for half an hour,
If we used that wonderful power,
There'd be peace on earth, we'd thank God above
For giving us the strength and capacity to love.

Heatwave

The sun is shining down from above,
Bringing with it a sense of peace and love.
But on days such as this
Its oppressive heat you can hardly miss,
No fresh air whatsoever.
I can hardly wait for an end to this weather,
Bring back the fresh, cold air,
A cool breeze blowing through my hair.
No more unbearably hot days and sticky nights,
Wake up feeling cool and fresh in the morning light.
People and their pets roaming through the park,
Cats contentedly purring and dogs giving a playful bark.
So thanks to the weather man who finally gave
A cheerful declaration of an end to this heatwave.

Halloween

Ghouls, goblins, ghosts and a witch,
Phantoms and beasts of the night,
Creepy crawlies that make you itch,
Werewolves who howl at the full moon's light,
Vampires who drink their victims' blood,
Stories told to give our children a fright,
Of zombies rising out of the mud,
On this the scariest of all nights.

Armistice

The war was ended,
'Twas finally over.
Returning from the trenches,
Our brave men pulled in to Dover:
Soldiers tired, battered and traumatized
At having witnessed carnage before their very eyes
On the battlefields of Flanders.
Buried deep below
Are those whom we loved and those we didn't know,
For death doesn't distinguish who's foe and who's friend,
It snaps at your heels and catches you in the end.
So on this day of remembrance and peace,
We thank God for the call for fighting to cease,
And even though this day may be bittersweet and sad,
That we survived at all we surely must be glad,
For we fought for peace, liberty and truth,
For freedom for children to live out their youth
In a world full of beauty, love and joy,
Peace for every man, woman, girl and boy.
So on this day of remembrance think on this:
Many men fought and died to bring us Armistice.

Winter

Snow is falling all around,
A blanket of white upon the ground.
Children throwing balls of snow,
Their rosy faces all aglow,
Going sledding through the park,
Out all hours playing 'til dark.
Building a snowman in the yard,
Making one is not very hard,
And to make sure your little ones don't start to cry,
For a nose you use a carrot and buttons for eyes.
And when it gets too dark to play,
You say to the children: "Let's call it a day."
So when that's all done and you're all warm indoors,
Sitting by the fire with hot chocolate and S'mores,
Those chocolate marshmallow sweets,
They're very delicious, succulent treats,
Whether roasting them over an open fire or in the oven,
You either hate 'em or you love 'em.
And when all is quiet and the children are tucked up in bed,
You turn off the lights and lay down your head,
Dream of the days when there's sunnier skies,
Warmth in the air and bright light in your eyes.
But even though you prefer hot summers, your children like winter best,
When the snow is falling and they put the weather to the test.
And even though you'd prefer to be wrapped up warm in the house,
You venture outdoors like a timid little mouse
To watch the children having a wonderful time,
They think the snow is so very sublime.
So thanks be to God for Winter, for the snow and the cold,
But you can't wait for Spring when flowers bloom and sun shines gold.
Green grass is everywhere you look around,
No blanket of white upon the ground.

Christmas

December 25th a great time of year,
Full of fun and laughter and a good lot of cheer.
Garlands of tinsel wrapped round the tree
Hung with ornaments, holly and ivy.
Presents grouped around under the tree,
Children eagerly awaiting their gifts,
Their smiling faces are not to be missed
When they rip off the paper and reveal what they've got,
It's a sight to behold that will mean a lot
Of happiness, joy and a lot of pleasure,
For the children are happy playing with their new found treasures,
And whilst they are playing you can crack open the wine
To go with the turkey roast when you dine.
And when round the table at the end of the meal
When the last morsel is eaten, to show how you feel,
Crackers are pulled, glasses are clinked,
And when all is done dishes are all piled in the sink.
Now bellies are full and silence resumed,
The family retires to the living room.
Turn on the box to watch the Queen's speech
And looking around at the children you say unto each:
"We've had a good time with plenty of cheer,
We wish you a Merry Christmas and a Happy New Year."

Christmas (II)

Christmas is a time of love, peace and joy,
Goodwill to every man, woman, girl and boy:
A fire blazing in the living room grate,
A tree for all the family to decorate
With lights, baubles and tinsel too.
Brightening the season for me and for you
Christmas tunes playing on that cassette,
Presents galore for all the family, and yet,
For all this pomp and circumstance,
All the festivities and the merry dance,
We should all remember the true meaning of the day,
When the baby away in a manger did lay.
To Mary the virgin mother so pure and so meek,
The Archangel Gabriel did come to speak:
"This baby thou hold in thine arms so dear
Shall be visited by pilgrims from far and from near."

And so came three kings who from the Orient were
Received, bringing gifts of Gold, Frankincense and Myrrh,
And soon all knew of the holy birth
That filled almost everyone with joy and mirth.
For Jesus Christ our saviour was born
On that ever so cold December morn.
And so while you're celebrating this time of the year,
And the children are waiting for Santa and his reindeer to appear,
Remember to give thanks to God for what you receive
On this the day after Christmas Eve.

Birthday

Birthdays come but once a year:
Celebrations full of fun, laughter and cheer.
The party lasts from six until twelve,
Next morning you wake up feeling like hell,
For you were plied with drinks for six hours straight,
That's why you can't remember getting home so late.
Your hangover's lethal, it feels so very bad,
Like your head's being hit with hammers, it's driving you mad.
Your hangover cure is supposed to work quick,
Instead of making you feel really sick.
So let this be a lesson to you:
Going teetotal's the right thing to do.
It keeps you sober, you have a clear head,
You don't wake in the morning, laid up in bed.
You remember family and friends and their own special way
Of throwing a party to celebrate your birthday.

THE DEMON DRINK

The Party

Gin, vodka and a whisky called Bell's
These are some of the drinks that you know so well,
Along with red, white and rosé wines,
Oh the taste is so very divine.
Beer, lager or maybe a shandy,
Or anything with alcohol in comes in handy
When you're throwing a party for family and friends
To make sure the jollities never come to an early end.
Put out some nibbles such as peanuts and crisps,
Or maybe you prefer to have Nachos and dips.
But for the designated drivers soft drinks will do:
There's lemonade, Pepsi and fruit juices too.
And when the party's over and you clean up the mess,
When everyone's gone and you have no more guests,
You're happy, you're cheerful, your laughter is hearty,
For you realise you've just thrown a fabulous party.

Alcohol

Wine, whiskey, vodka and gin,
They're so addictive, to drink them is surely a sin.
Beer, lager, brandy and sherry,
Your head is spinning, you feel oh so merry.
And just to prove that you are able,
You get up and start dancing on the table.
The night begins to take its toll,
For your headache is due to partaking of too much alcohol.

The New Old Woman

There is an old woman who used to drink like a fish
Her favourite meal was always an alcohol-laced dish.
From morning until night she'd be seen having a drink
And gradually from that bar stool she would sink,
And in the mornings when she would awake,
The room would be spinning, she'd have a splitting headache.
But after downing some aspirins she'd be back at the bar,
Yet she knew that her drinking had been a problem thus far.
So come the new year she vowed to make a change
And live a healthier life which to her seemed quite strange.
So gone are the sherry, gin, brandy and wine,
They have been replaced by soft drinks which taste just fine.
And now whenever you pass her out in the street,
She's friendly, she's cheerful, she's steady on her feet.
And when you speak to her she doesn't slur her words,
Her voice is the sweetest thing that you've ever heard.

The Old Man and His Drinking

There lives an old man who has worked hard all his life,
To be able to provide for his family for fear of upsetting his wife.
That's why every weekend for fifty years he could be found at the local inn,
To avoid being constantly nagged at by a wife whose patience had worn pretty thin.
For although he'd earned a fair old wage,
It was never enough to stop her flying into a fit of rage,
So when it came time to stagger home from the pub,
She'd be there to nag him for coming in late and drunk.
And so it went on and somehow he resisted
The urge to throttle her for strife that between them existed.
He was beginning to really fear for his life each time he entered the room,
For she'd started throwing all the knives, forks and spoons.
Until the one night when it had gone past one a.m.,
The old woman at home was fuming about his lateness coming betwixt them.
He lumbered through the front door, coat dripping wet and boots covered in mud,
He realised far too late that she'd be after his blood,
So as soon as he'd entered the kitchen stinking of booze,
He was prepared for a fight which he knew he would lose.
Her fury that raged right through the house
Was enough to frighten even the bravest little mouse,
And although he shall end his life behind bars,
He cannot find any comfort in the knowledge that she'd pushed him too far.
That's why he can never ever begin to explain
The amount of stress or the emotional pain
Of having had to struggle to co-exist
With a nagging wife who drove him to drink until he was pissed.
Up until that ever so tragic night,
When the wife was at home waiting to pick a fight,
Before her nagging had even started,
Already feeling exhausted and down-hearted,
He picked up the first thing that came to hand,
And on the top of her head that weapon did land.

And now she is waiting beyond the grave
To have a go at him, to rant and rave,
But he is safe and sound in his peaceful jail cell,
For his nagging wife is probably rotting in Hell.
So before every man out there lumbers himself with a wife,
Just think: "Is she worth all the hassle, the trouble and strife?"
'Cause if he stops and takes a few minutes to think,
He'd be better off living with the demon drink.

REFLECTIONS

The Ghost in the Mirror

It was a cold, cold day,
The wind howling down the passageway,
The echoing creek
Of floorboards under feet,
As I made my way
Through that dark passageway.
As I wandered from room to room,
I shivered in the gloom,
When I heard someone shout:
"Look out, look out, look out!"
Nervously I turned to see
Someone staring back at me.
I asked her her name,
She replied, "We are both but the same."
As I walked toward her,
I was surprised by my reaction,
'Cause in front of me was a mirror
And in it was my reflection.

Chocolate

White, milk, dark or plain,
The taste's delicious all the same.
Bounty, Twix, Snickers and Mars,
To find anything tastier you'd have to search far.
Maltesers, Buttons, Smarties or Rolo,
You share with a friend 'cause you can't bear to eat solo.
And even though you eat too many and it may rot your teeth,
You ignore all the signs, you just don't want to give up these treats.
And your belly is growing, you're putting on too much weight,
You've ignored all the warning signs and now it's too late,
But there comes a stage in life when it's passed time to care,
When you can hardly fit into your clothes, you even struggle to put on underwear.
But you've got enough worries to fill up your plate,
To give a damn about salad which is something you hate,
And eating a little of what you like doesn't do you much harm,
Or so you believe until you're being carted off to the fat farm.
And when you've lost a few stones off of your weight
You can enjoy again some deliciously wholesome chocolate.

Cakes

Mr Kipling makes
Exceedingly deliciously scrumptious cakes,
Whether they're covered with chocolate or filled with jam,
Or maybe you'd prefer them topped with marzipan.
There're cakes that are made for special occasions,
There're cakes for Christmas, birthday and anniversary celebrations,
There're small, large, tiered and cupcakes too,
Round or square. Which one do I want to get for you?
Sponge cake full of raspberry preserve or a cake made with fruit?
Which should I choose? Which one would suit?

The best friend whose acquaintance I was lucky to make,
So I've got to choose you the most perfect of cakes.

Wanderlust

Through cold gales blowing into my face,
I'll trudge on desperately in my haste
To win this marathon of a race,
I mustn't stop to rest, there's no time to waste.

As I look ahead I can see the finish,
But however fast I go, the distance doesn't seem to diminish.
The rain comes down heavy and fast:
How long is this downpour going to last?

And finally this deluge from the sky ceases,
The sun shines down which is something that pleases.
I look straight ahead and I'm glad to say
That I'm almost there, it's taken half a day.

And now I quicken up my pace,
To win will be my saving grace.
And with a smile on my face I look around and say,
"Maybe I'll run faster another day."

And now I realise there's nothing that I can't do
If I put my mind to it and think it through,
For now that I've raced and my opponents have eaten my dust,
I have discovered that I now have the wanderlust.

Cruising

Never in your life did you think you would be
Cruising away on the deep blue sea,
On board a ship sailing to distant lands.
Life at sea is oh so grand:
There's friends to be made with passengers and crew,
And there's always a friendly "How do you do?"
There's dishes of so much succulent food,
You eat every last mouthful 'cause leaving any would surely be rude.
And when it's time to go home, the holiday's ended,
It's sad to leave behind the people you've befriended,
But there'll always be another time
When you're sailing on a different line,
Whether it be P&O, Fred Olsen or Cunard.
Meeting like-minded people is not so hard,
And when it's all over you can look back on the years,
And cherish those memories you hold so dear
Of sailing away on the big blue yonder,
And looking back you may well wonder
When did the cruising days come to an end,
And what became of those wonderful friends?
'Cause there's one memory you never shall lose,
And that's of the first time you went on a cruise.

Dreams

When I go to sleep at night I dream
Of warm, sandy beaches and cold ice creams,
Or of boarding a ship to sail the seas,
Standing on deck, hair blowing in the breeze,
Dancing the night away under the stars,
Having a last drink before they close the bars.
Fun, gaiety, love and laughter,
Happiness and joy is all I am after,
No threat of holidays called off due to COVID 19,
'Cause diseases and viruses don't exist in my dreams.

The Dream

Through rain, through sleet,
Through lightning sheet,
You shall not stop those weary feet,
Running, running through the streets
In search of the man you're destined to meet.
He's tall, he's handsome and very charming
And when he smiles it's quite disarming,
And when he takes you in his arms
You're about to surrender to his fatal charms,
When suddenly you hear a knock…
You wake up startled, full of shock.
You realise that, as wonderful as he may have seemed,
That man was nothing but a dream.

Good v Evil

The prince of evil can be found
Thousands of miles underground.
He feeds off people's violence and greed
Doesn't give a damn about those in need.
'Destruction' is Satan's middle name,
But he's never around to take the blame;
He leaves all kinds of mayhem in his wake,
Devastation for devastation's sake.
But there's less evil in the world than there is good,
Kindness in many neighbourhoods.
If we all were kind for just one day,
The Devil would be vanquished, sent away,
And in God's kingdom we shall be forever ordained,
Peace and happiness throughout the world will reign.

Life After Death

As I lie in bed I'm wide awake,
Wishing to get rid of this incessant ache,
For even though I know they've gone away,
I see my loved ones every day:
Parents, siblings, cousins and pets,
I see each and every one of them, and yet
When I finally take my last breath,
I'll leave this world knowing there's life after death.
Even though they're gone I feel a dull pain,
But I know I shall meet them all again.
So please don't mourn my passing for too long,
Just think of me and perhaps sing a happy song.
For although I'm dead not alive, I can be found
In every joyous moment and happy sound.
My spirit shall forever be around,
In the air and on the ground.
And if ever you should feel bereft,
Close your eyes and see that I never really left,
'Cause at the end of my life as at the start,
I'll forever be right there inside your heart.

About the Author

When Michelle was three and a half, whilst out with her mother watching the local carnival, they proceeded to cross the road whilst the traffic was stationary. A coach drove backwards, resulting in Michelle being crushed against a car. She sustained severe brain damage and other injuries. She was not expected to live, so to survive and be able to write poetry is nothing short of amazing.